traveling women

by

opal palmer adisa
&
devorah major

daughters of yam

Jukebox Press
Oakland, California

Acknowledgements

Grateful acknowledgment is made to the editors of the following magazines and anthologies in which some of these poems were previously published:
San Francisco Poetry Quarterly
Practicing Angel
Compages
Black Scholar

Cover Art: Woody Johnson
Cover Design: Tumikia Wata
Book Design: Tumikia Wata
 with Devorah Major
Typesetting and Layout: East Bay Data Base
Photographs: David Major

Copyright ©1989
by Opal Palmer Adisa
and Devorah Major

Published by: Jukebox Press
 3717 Market Street
 Oakland, California 94608

All Rights Reserved

Library of Congress Catalog Number:
89-083489
- ISBN 0-932693-01-6

Printed in the United States

What is happening to the daughters of yam? Seem like they just don't know how to draw up the powers from the deep like before. Tell me, how do I welcome this daughter home to the world.

    Toni Cade Bambara,
    The Salt Eaters

DEDICATED

to the griots
those seekers of words
those who know
that to put words
to memory
is to let history live
is to continue the promise
of our ancestors
is to provide a place
for our children to grow
for the children
who we must
teach the words
so they can continue
and advance our soul-force
those who
use words
and know the meaning
and flavor the color
of their voices
and stamp the shape
of words
on other's memory
the words' seekers
to our parents
to our lovers/husbands
to our children
to the people who inspire
us and without whom
these words would not be possible
   to life itself
and the total freeing
of the african continent
to freedom...

opa

TABLE OF CONTENTS

dedicated	4
traveling women	9
the word	12
history lesson	17
passage	18
african cosmology	22
sea shell	24
my work speaks to those other women	28
woman's cycle	30
we bleed	31
ancestry 1	33
rape as it relates to incest	35
womb renting	37
no women no cry	39
women's agronomy	41
the drum is the heart	44
executing the righteous	46
test run	47
war	50
today's grandmother	53
grenada sunset	57
resistance	60
jazz me	64
death and ritual	65
let them laugh	67
first sounds	70
history of a 'merican word	72
children without crime	74
black woman I	76
conversation with mother	81
cracker jacks	83
what we gonna do 'bout dem youth?	86
the real black beauty	89
longing	92
living/hating	93
lovers	95
the beginning	96
sharing everything	97
i want to	98
travel notes	101

OPENING

DAUGHTERS OF YAM/
TRAVELING WOMEN

we walk streets
looking on byways
and through trees
we find our mothers
one of us drinks blue
names herself daughter
of yemoja
produces new life
weaving her liquid feet
in the belly of the ocean
throwing coconuts wherever
she wanders
the other drinks yellow-orange
fans her coquettish manner
free
spinning a web
where men dance in her honor
she has who she wishes
but all wait on her love
for her name is oshun

daughters of yam
traveling women
on the road
where there are more
maps to read
than people to hear
we pierce ears   stretch lips
taking time to listen
to worn tales of elders
remembering them
as they flow out
black and true
playing hide and seek
with children
who whisper
fantastic dreams
to invisible playmates
sifting across the news of today
discovering promises next to pain
daughters of yam/
traveling women

on roads
carrying the rich soil
of africa
between our breasts
pausing at every crossroad
examining road signs
deciphering
the pebbles of sand
the heels of feet
left in gravel tracks
recording all the dead
celebrating all marriages
offering libation for the births
nursing the sick
bringing love
our blue and yellow skirts
sweeping the dust
as we travel
we daughters of yam
on the road
collecting refuse
varnishing streets
burnishing trees
pruning fruits and plowing fields
pruning fruits and plowing fields

    we are daughters of yam
traveling women
come to you
with a part of
our history

opa/dm

HISTORY

THE WORD

    in the beginning
was the word
the word
the word
    it comes up
from my bowels
the word
the word
laced in pasteurized
blending of all

    i have ingested
the word
the word

    it comes up
these words
slide from my throat
after i receive
a thump in my back
the word
    in the beginning
was the word
from the navel
of my center
the word
trapped
on the roof of my mouth
between the crevices of my teeth
the word
the word
    the word
lost
knocking at mouths
twisted from years of mis-stories
the word
    shaping meaning
    back into
    the vowels/consonants
    the word
    before it was spoken

the word
that i try
to speak
the word that
cries
the word
that destroys
like hurricane gilbert
that levelled my home
the word

in the beginning
was the word
i try to find it
render it free
like this freedom
i've been seeking
the word
that lost its voice
in the cargo of a ship
perfumed in feces
and the confused
state of a people
tricked/lied to
deceived by greed
and shinny glass
the word
that now stutters/stammers
        the word
        the word
in the beginning
before
woman and man
laid together
before the race
was set in motion
the word was god
and ruled the land
the word was the dream
and made day follow night
the word was love
and was seen
in the blue-tipped wings
of the jay

                    the word
                    the word
in the beginning
before
we discovered
duplicity/to take words
like spit
to tease/trap/defile
my word was the order
and in the order
was the word
                    the word
                    the word

the word
that sings
i mean to shape
back its form
find the house in which
it once lived
give back the truth
listen to what
i know i must say

from the beginning
was the word
and the word was me
the word echoes
the notes of the
talking drum
echoes the love
of beating hearts
echoes the rhythm
of dancing feet

the beginning
all i had was
what i gave
i gave my word
and it was understood

the word
was respected
the word
was the light

          the word
          the word
now i stumble
my fingers
grope dirt
trying to replant
the soil in which
the word has taken refuge
the word
crying beside
my dead child
in the homelands
of south africa
the word
that is sown
in the moving lips
of these homeless street walkers
those beggars of selfhood
the word
that my not yet
four year old
uses to spur me/taunt me
demand of me

the word
that has lost its feet
and whose leathery soles
no longer leave foot prints

the word
that those kidnapped
children all over
the world voice
this is my name
where is my mommy
why are these people
keeping me from my mommy

the word
that those silent parents
with pregnant eyes
weave in their heads
questioning their negligence
reaching for hands that
do not respond

voices that do not
cry out in the night
seeking comfort

the word
that politicians use
to make mockery
of the plunder
the power mania

in the beginning
was the word
             the word
             the word
that i keep seeking
the word
still in my navel
the word
nurtured in my menses
the word
that lives always
at the edge of my
finger prints
the word
that i still must find
to speak
the word
             the word
             the word

opa

HISTORY LESSON

before we became
yoruba, ashanti, fulani, mandingo
jones , freeman, washington, x
before we became
christian, moslem, yoruba,
voodoo, macumba, santaria.
before we became
black against brownblack
against yellowblack against
brother against sister
against self,
we were one.
before the tribe,
before the temple,
before the name
we were one.
and when we were one
crops grew each summer
winter was a time of rain
and young love making.
when we were one
we harvested dreams
and knew the universe's secrets
and knew the universe's secrets
when we were one we spoke
not of clenched teeth survival
but of dance filled celebration.
we held god in the spaces
between our joints
and together we would sing
and together we would sing
and together we would sing.

dm

PASSAGE

no fare
was requested
no seat
was granted
just the feel
of my breasts
the luster
of my supple skin

no fare
was demanded
just the strength
of my milky teeth
the arch of my back
the wide expanse
of my womb

no fare
was stipulated
just the silence
of my rape
and endurance
the nurturing of their
children

no fare
no even exchange
of food for water
blood for pain
curse for sin
toil for endurance
just my invisibility
invincibility
inversion
invidiousness
inviolability

no fare
no paper
passed through
my hands
no beads
placed on

my neck
no cloth
draped my body
no fare
no barter
no bargain
i came involuntary
i could not invoke
and my gods
went inward
inside that place
where we take
ourselves
to quell
the taste of memory

no fare
only the flitting
of images
that fade to dust
the ocean clear blue
and wicked
the taste of salt
other than my own
the sounds
not of drums
but drum-like
thunder of cries
talking of aches
rumble of defeat
echo of a passing

no fare
each time
the smell of yam
fufu
okra
red mud
wrapped themselves
around my body
a lash said
i was irascible

no fare
no payment

my home felled
my alter burned
just the nightmarish
replay
water splashing
foam in the air
angry white
swirling
my geography away
the splash
and swell
like a knave
that lives always
on my lid

no fare
days after
months after years
after the first time
the puking smell
and dinner of salt
the vulgar assault
to my ears
so i flee
from the sea

no fare
no passage
just passing
into
ionosphere
where cotton
was never soft
nor cane sweet
where white
was never pure
and the sun
was a syphilitic leech
who pulled at my skirt
and exploded fire
in my womb

no fare
just transformation
of colors

no fare
just renaming
no fare
just here
now
me
bits of pieces
mixture of variegated
rags held together
by air
will
and the memory
that has faded
but won't die
too stubborn
like me
to forget
the sound
of the sea
white foam
swelling
rising up
to carry me across
history
to home

no fare
no fare
no fare
for me
no fare

opa

AFRICAN COSMOLOGY

in that place
in that time

when the seeds we swallowed
planted themselves
in moist red folds
began to suck sweet womb juices
to grow root veins
translucent skins
pushed out our bellies in mounds
that undulated life as we bent
over spring seedlings.

when the birth entrails
were bathed in palm wine
buried in moss filled earthen altars
beneath baobab trees spawned
from feces of orangutan bowels.
in that time
when seasons' comings
reflected clocks' time
and seasons' passing
recorded time's ignorance

in that age when god was found
in flowing river beds' algae
sung to on stretched goat skins
bathed in blood and milk
from a white haired ewe.
then we understood life
as an undying seed
cousin to the wind
child of the ocean
mother of the earth.

in that place
in that time

in that humid sweated
plant filled land
of birth and passing
rebirth and changes
cycles/world unseen

and remembered
in candle lit ceremony
we knew not death
and we could
not be destroyed.

dm

SEA SHELL

my lips
spread
my labial
parts
my legs
open
my arms
encircle

the mouth
of the shell
records the sea
for dreams

trap it
to your ears
watch it part
spread to
the sea
tumble out
bone hard
and soft
rings of lines
twisted
into knots
for years

my labial
washed ashore
pink with memory
the roar and crow
of the sea
the breath and depth
of its heat
the shell
carries its meat
inside
deep like
the liver of my womb
watch it spread
swish, soar, swirl
hear the roaring cry
that connects you

to me
us to them
we to the distant
swept ashore
carried to another place
the shell of the sea
stores our memories
place us to your ears
hear our chatter
cry of drowned lands
unrecognized laughter
my lips part
hold water
my arms tremble
press back tide
my labial contracts
water squeezed
into vapors of pools
the taste of which
stirs a tomorrow
i would rather
not know
generations drowned
walking back home
on the ripple of the waves

sea shell
washed ashore
relic of
the middle passage
the slave trade
bodies tossed
at sea
the hold
moaning
the chained voices
ringing
competing
with the splash
of the waves
that crash
crescending
waves
wail
decay

insisting on lives
feet that know
the road of the waves

mourners of tears
frigid flight
the continuous echo
trembling water
my legs part
for your entrance

opa

WOMEN

MY WORK SPEAKS TO THOSE OTHER WOMEN

i am
wo/man
i woo, i walk, i wail, i talk.

my poetry
are legs and breasts
thighs and swinging behinds;
the poems cry of neglect,
laugh with the sun,
dance under the blazing flamboyant trees
raise dust with bare feet
and use the hem of dresses to wipe sweat,
wipe odor from brows and sweating
underarms

these poems are women
reeking of the blood
that drips monthly
that some women put in their food
to keep what's theirs theirs
singing of troubled locked in boxes
that females are always left to guard

these poems are about women
who have always worked
in soil, at river banks
in beds, in kitchens, on street corners
working without writing down their poems
working so that others can study and
write about them
working because they must

these poems are of the *Shes*
she is there
for the supporting,
for the unplugged microphones,
to produce;
she is there
and gives birth of new poems
some stored in the after-birth
some postponed/denied by the pill,
the bush tea,

the condom, the withdrawal, the abortion;
these are women's poems
defined by their roundness,
their backs tall and hard,
their lips pulled tight
to quiet screams

these are female poems
wet with vaginal juice
and the loving eyes
that women keep for each other

in each shape of a leaf
in every song of the moon
with the rising waters
each is a poem
feminine define
these poems are herstory

opa

WOMAN'S CYCLE

with the earth
i share kinship.
i am daughter
of the rivers
mother of the
waterfalls.
it is me
who circles
from rain cloud
to mountain
to iced streams
clear lakes
frothing ocean
returning to the sky.
it is me who gives
forth blood
each month returning
myself to myself.

dm

WE BLEED

i want to
get rid of
this blood
every month
i want to
stop the
bloated feeling
the low-depression
the sensitivity
and bleeding

i want to
get rid of
this blood
every month

the song i sing
knows no limit
except for the blood
that drips down
my legs
soils
my pretty dress
slows me down

i want to
get rid of
this blood
every month
maybe it's true
that's how they caught us
tripped us up
took our power
they smelled
the blood oozing
out of us
with no soil
to catch it
and fear
was fixed in their eyes
and they marked us
by the moon
so i want to

get rid of
this blood
every month
i want to stop
the bleeding
the bloated feeling
the swings in mood
the lost of myself
that drips away
with only compact tissue
to catch me

i want to
get rid of
this bleeding
to keep
all of myself
to not be
tripped up by the moon
to be free again
to be a warrior
to walk naked
dawn to month
to not soil
my dress
to not continuously lose
parts of myself
in red liquid
dripping

stop the bleeding.

opa

ANCESTRY 1

she is inside of me.
she pushes at my womb
stretches my tongue
remembers.

she is here, inside
pulling against the chains
diving into the cold white foam
offering herself to yemoja.
in chains making herself ebo
that the captain would die
a pox-filled swollen death,
the boat never find its shore.

she is inside close
pushing her child out
between measured breaths
kissing away the soft cream
that coats its tiny fingers
fills the crevices between its toes.
bringing it to her breast for
one moment
and then rolling over it soft
until sweet breath is trapped
in new lungs
and the life that is free
returns to the source.

she is here
in the heavy branches
of the iroko tree
weaving silence around her heart
as her brothers are driven
into slave lines
whipped into mutants.

she has survived it all.
she lives.
she has kept a piece
of her song alive.
she pounds yams and sings
hums to the noonday sun
drinks sweet water

wraps her limbs in blue cottons
remembering the night skies
and joins the circle dance.

the heels of her feet are cracked.
her hands are wings
as they sow harvest seeds.
her feet stamp on each turn
as the music bids her, rock her head
smile and sing, ire, we are blessed
alafia.

she sparkles in my eyes.
she lives.
i did not ask her to come
to this shell
parched skin
city weak limbs.
she comes because she lives.
she makes time her garden and
nurtures each new body
so that she may go home
one day, one year, one century past.

she lives inside of me
and prays daily
for tranquility.

*yemoja is the yoruba godforce/orisha
over the ocean.
ebo means sacrifice, usually, but not
always, of a live animal.
iroko tree is a hardwood tree brought
 to this hemisphere at the request of slaves.

dm

RAPE AS IT RELATES TO INCEST

(dedicated to the boy who accidentally
 raped his mother
and his friends who shared the moment.)

hey, manchild/boy so young/so strong
when you took her/tore into her middle
when your hand pressed against her mouth
and she bit blood and hate
when you pulled aside her cotton skirt
jammed into her iron tensed birthway
as you twisted her womb
as she beat your back
as she cried/as she begged
as you came in thick globs of cream
spread them around her fertileness
how could you forget that in africa/times
she was of an age that would
have made her your
sister/sister you would have called her
as together you danced the harvest festival.

you, manchild/boy struggling
against the times
bent from the storm
eyes blindfolded with clouds
of pain and madness
when you grabbed her from behind
when she feebly clawed against your
muscled hands/when you scratched
through layers of
mildew and cloth to that center
preserved for god since her husband passed
when she bled as she prayed
when you trembled inside her
how could you forget
in long past africa/times
you would have called her grandmother
bowed as you entered her home as she
shared with you kola nuts and sweet tea.

manchild/boy as you threw the coat
over her head
never having seen her lips move or eyes smile

35

as you spread sweat into her tears
thrust hard into her middle
as she bled and turned to acid your life juices
how could you forget that in once
remembered africa/times
she would have been called mother
in africa/times it would have been your life.

when you rape
would be man/punching power into strange
women's orifices
it is always a family affair.

dm

WOMB RENTING

mary
           mary whitehead
what were you thinking
when you signed away
your right
to the life you were nurturing
inside your dark womb

did you think
you had choices
that this was a free land
that slavery was a misnomer
that you were a matriarch
and could oppose the men
of this society
when male and money
were at stake

mary
           mary whitehead
did you think
children were for sale
a life you helped to create
was worth $10,000
and that you could rent
your womb
to provide for your two children
and abusive alcoholic husband

what were you thinking
when you first felt melissa kick
against your rib
when she made somersault
in your stomach
when you squeezed her out
the blood that covered her
the pain that you nursed
in your veins
did you think
william stern, biochemist
and elizabeth stern, pediatrician
would allow you to keep the child
they paid for

did you think
you woman/poor
could stand up in the courts of law
that judge/man
regard your womb as anything other
than a receptacle to plant his seed
did you think his wife, barren woman
that she is would understand
that if she wanted a child so badly
and couldn't have one
then you
who grew life strong
would need to cradle your child

but what about melissa
in all of this
do children need money to grow
well and strong
to be sensitive/objective adults
has money prevented children
from being abused, unloved

   mary
               mary whitehead
what are you thinking
what are you feeling
does melissa haunt you
point her finger
and accuse you of being
a baby-machine
a seller
a buyer
a consumer

   mary
               mary whitehead
may oshun wash your hair
yemoja sponge your body
you can't pick a rose
and not prick your finger
mary
               mary whitehead
who holds your dreams

   opa

NO WOMEN NO CRY

in africa the saying is:
a man is nothing without a woman.
he cannot be chief
and when his breath
leaves him, his name
will be knocked into the earth
forgotten as his flesh

we women don't cry
we carry pain
in our bosoms
our stomachs bulge
pregnated with sorrow
we guard tears
like a dam
for if we were to shed one drop
we couldn't stop
and we wouldn't have been able
to fight the portuguese in the congo
the english in portland hills of jamaica
prisoners and derelicts of europe
in the americas

if just one salt
had run down our cheeks
the pyramids wouldn't have been built
and the 60,000,000 africans
who drowned, starved and were killed
in the usurpation of the continent
the middle passage
wouldn't even be a memory

women don't cry
we don't cry
mothers don't cry
when their husbands creep through
the back door
while they remain with a stone stare
to sing freedom in the enemy's face,
sisters don't cry
when they see their brothers
strung up, mutilated
daughters don't cry

when a moment's rape
alters their future
no women don't cry
we just hold it in
in the crevices of our teeth
in our wombs,
under our armpits,
in the loops of our ears
we women don't cry
we only weep and wail
in our rocking
that's why we talk to ourselves
and build more lives

opa

WOMEN'S AGRONOMY

we grow things.
two flowers
petals drifting
dance within,
loam thickens walls
turns us round and thick.
we grow things.
insects which shuttle
across invisible layers of flesh
pollinate our auras
as mushrooms flourish in sadness
pungent and cushioned.
we grow children, poems,
madness, witchcraft,
even volcanoes, at times.
we grow things
from the earth of spirit
the rain of blood
dirt, spit and
tenacity, we grow
gardens within ourselves.
when mother nature
looks into her mirror
to see her fields fallow
or harvests full
she eyes our gardens
and smiles.

dm

POLITICS

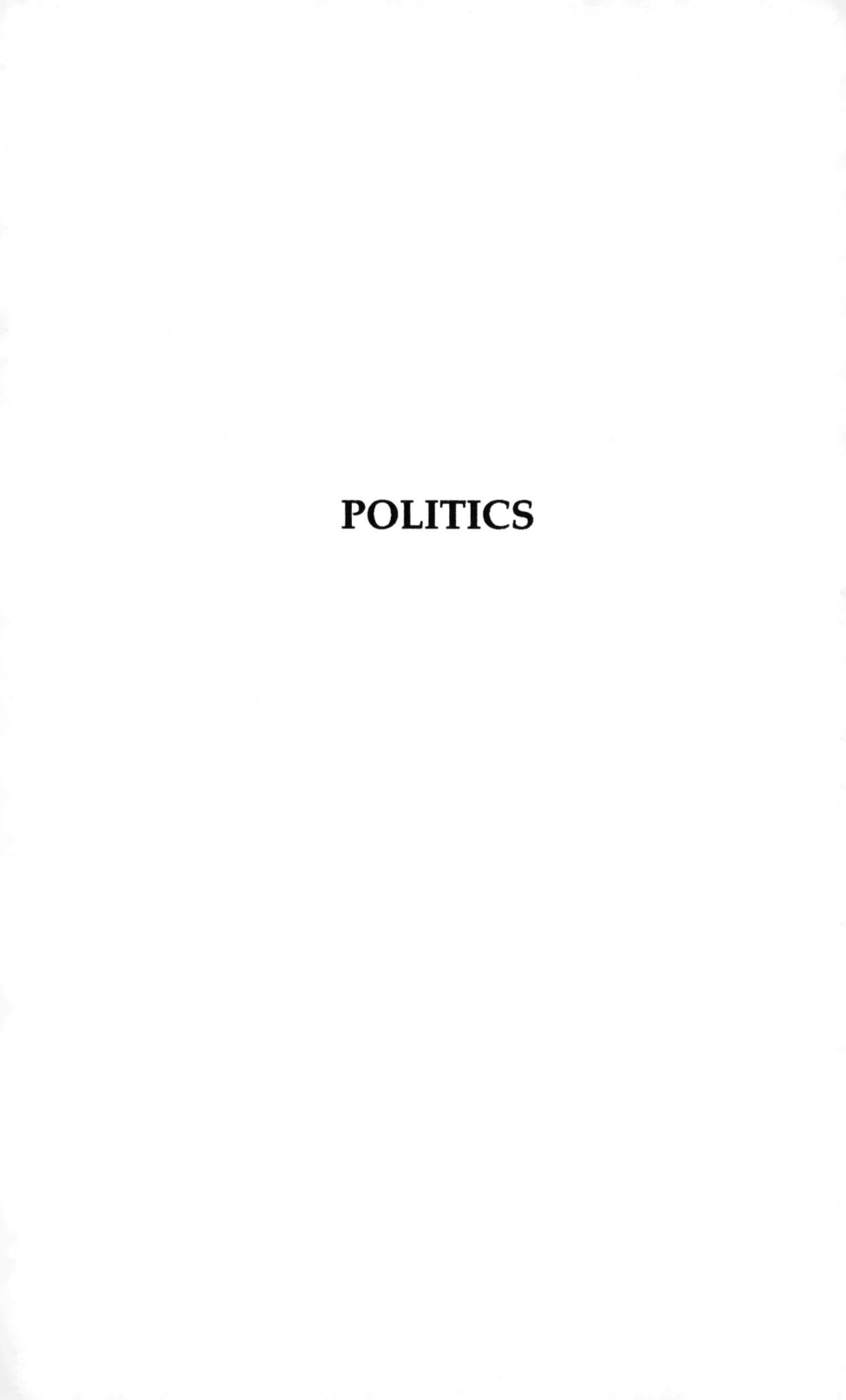

THE DRUM IS THE HEART

                the drums
                beat...

kinfolks
in africa land
do you mourn us
all us sold for profit
all us kidnapped
spread throughout
the rest of the world
all us thrown overboard
to avoid fines
all us drowned
walking back
home to you--
to africa
all us lost/dead
in the hold
all us bartered
for beads, rum, oranges

                the drums
                beat us...

kinfolks
in africa land
i have been singing
your songs
nursing my wounds
to come to you
but you
who were not
swapped for trinkets
you who remained
close to our ancestors
do you mourn us
pour libation
go on pilgrimage
to the ocean
ask yemoja/goddess of the water
to protect us/watch over us
do you weep
for those of us

sacrificed
those of us
who survived
by creating
spirituals/blues/odes

   the hearts
   beat...

kinfolks in africa land
seek us
kill a chicken
and drain the blood
for us
pay homage
in remembrance
some of us
were traded
some of us
were murdered
some of us
lost touch with who
we were/are
all of us
are continuing...

   drums
   beat us onward
   carry our spirits home
   beat on drums
   beat on hearts...

opa

EXECUTING THE RIGHTEOUS

(dedicated to three condemned
ANC revolutionaries)

they will hang you.
they will read their morning papers,
wonder at their servants' morose silence.
they will swallow fatty desperate sex.
they will try to relax.
they will hang you three,
and give birth to three hundred more.
they will cushion their turgid dreams
with american imported whiskey,
and they will belch
thick fetid fear.

dm

TEST RUN

inside america
is a sore
that has festered
leaving maggots
fat

and blackbirds
are shot off the
fence

atlanta was a
test run
a test run
a test run
leaving our children
dead

inside america
is slavery
400 years
continuing on
into the present

blackbirds are
shot off
the fence

go north
for freedom
go north
for jobs
go north
to kiss the
statue of
someone else's
liberty

1930's riot
go north

inside america
is a sore
that is racism/discrimination

the master
has a new dress
and the new master
lives up north
where he has always been
bernard hugo goetz, et al
lives up north
go north
for freedom
go north
black/boys/men
shot
strung up
terrorized
murdered
disenfranchised
made to be the
scapegoat
the slave without
protection
a century
after slavery
was transformed
to urban ghettoization

atlanta was
a test run
a test run
a test run
leaving our children
dead

inside america
is a people
exiled from
the empire
they helped to build

inside america
is the atlantas
inside america is racism
black people
given the image
of the dream
to throw away their weapons

to abandon their beliefs
to surrender their children
to relinquish
the little control they
had over their lives

atlanta was
a test run
a test run
a test run

let's run for freedom
the new master is
everywhere
is pus inside
this sore
is pus
inside this
festering wound

black boys are shot
dead/wounded
murdered, lynched,
tracked/imprisoned
and my people
shuffle their feet
and move on

what can be done?

atlanta is a
sore not yet healed
blackbirds are still
being shot off the fence
their wings clipped
as they dive for food
so this blackbird
has learned to live
on air

opa

WAR

1. ancient ritual

one general proud
would tell the other general, also proud,
the story of his life
voicing some of the names of his people,
singing a phrase, pacing each verse
as memory and history would allow him.

the other would return arched tale
for cupped tale
outlining who begat and why
while speaking of the bounty of his land,
taking out pallet stroking green,
remembering umber sunsets

then the first would return the flourish
speaking quietly of the love he had
known, remembering precisely how
his hands fell
in the mounds and crevices how
she pulled herself around him
the pain in their leavings

and both their loins would become
warm and moist and their sword
would glisten in the red tinted sky
and they would each begin to stiffen
in the honoring of other passions
when only little deaths were welcomed,
until,
at last
they could say to each other
and to their troops
that they knew each
the other well.
following which
each stood and bowed
turned shoulders grazing the blue-black sky
as they returned to their mounts
to prepare for the next morning
when the war could now
properly begin.

i cannot hold on to the reasoning
why it is better death
how it makes a truer war
if knowing, instead of ignorance
remains prelude to killing.
is this why the ocean always moans?

2. parting

each general feared a woman's menses
would bath him in the seepage of war
redolent in the flesh it washed away
expanding in the flow
instead of becoming diminished
by a river of red.

each general feared a woman's blood
and would not touch her before battle
if the moon sat round upon her cheeks
cast shadows on her mood

3. sarge

now
years
having passed
he sits
legs agape
zipper always open
wilted flesh
propped out the
fly space.
he stares
at it
remembers
that
first
he took the man who
begged and whimpered
like a weak pussy
for his goddamn-son-of-a-bitch life instead
of facing death like a man

so when he stuck him through the belly
and watched him quiver around his knife
sarge got stiff and raped
the m.f.'s hole
calling him punkass
and woman.
then he arose
and to prove it was not a habit
but a legitimate act of war
he took each of the dead man's
remaining family
one
at
a
time
the daughter
the grandmother
and hours later tearing the baby from her
arms the mother
who bled around his penis
staring without tears
spitting her venom
like bullets onto his face
until
pulling his limp and
coated member from
her weeping channel
he began to doubt and feel shame.

ever since
he stares
and waits
waits for it to fall off
and ceases to haunt him
in the sallow gutter of his
memories.
the blood he rocks
and stares
it was the blood,
every time old sarge
pulls out his war stories
for one more look.

dm

TODAY'S GRANDMOTHER

(a promise to my daughter shola)

sometimes
when we speak a word
repeatedly
it becomes lost
why we're fighting
somehow gets confused
with guilt

we're taught
to know the enemy
sometimes
the enemy
becomes so intimate
we become the enemy
of ourselves
our people

do we know
whether we're engaged
in war/insurrection/revolution

these are different
not merely semantic
replacements of corruption
for color

sometimes
we speak a word
not knowing
its meaning
so victory
doesn't begin
to be the sound of
azania/namibia
and people
over the world
are vomiting blood
to achieve

out of the mountain
they came

53

locust
carrying on their heads
whispers of words
told to them
generations and generations
ago

they were warned
some will come
claim then transmute
beware
friendliness killed
as stupidity
generosity stolen
as lack of need

sometimes

when we speak
we speak a word
repeatedly
meaning gets lost

out of the forest
they came
dripping honey
to be ambushed
they were warned

i'm a mother today
twenty-five years
after tomorrow
i'll be a grandmother
rocking my daughter's children
on my knees
whispering words of
generation and generations
passed

i'll not disguise
spilled blood
bodies sprawled over soweto
mats of grass for dogs to scratch
their fleas on
they were warned

sometimes
we speak
we speak a word
repeatedly
not knowing the meaning

i'm not recounting
history
that thing which
no longer lives
i'm not naming
atrocities
that which still happens
they were warned

women deserve
the best or worst
of their men
sharing their beds
children need
the advantage or spoil
of a mother's hand
that sometimes sends
one's head spinning
or cradle one in comfort

they used to be warriors
not only men
women were bravest
they put food on tables

my grandchildren
are pulling my hair
their empty gums
suck their cheeks
imploring
no more no more
mass funerals
no more no more
killings
no more no more
bantu land

sometimes
when we speak

we speak a word
until it resounds
without meaning

my grandchildren
are calling
no more no more
divide and rule
no more no more
scavengers from the sea
no more no more
sacrifice
no more no more
biko
no more no more
winnie mandela
no more no more
nelson mandela
no more no more
people subjected
no more no more

sing on sing on
sometimes
we must speak
words that we mean

opa

GRENADA SUNSET

(for a war's beginning)

grenada, your beaches are swept
with gunboat grease, empty shells and blood.
where shall i send my dreams to live?

grenada, your beaches are white.
they blind my eyes.
your beauty sends chills
through my belly.
i shiver when you breathe
limping and wounded.

your people press their palms over
gaping holes shot through their freedom.
they twist tourniquets around your limbs,
which fall, dry, useless
against your flattened arteries.
grenada, how does a farmer kill
a flock of locusts?
how does a child escape a hive of wasps
circling, pointedly stinging?

it's clear: mercenaries come cheap these days.
even brothers can be made to kill brothers
for another stripe,
and a good retirement pension
after twenty years of looking glass journeys
from share cropper,
past unemployment statistic
direct to trained killer.
all the soldiers know of you
are your beaches, your people
burnt by the sun and painted with earth
and the way the rifles feel
wedged between their legs.

grenada, your beaches
are swept with blood and seaweed.
gun shells fall out of oysters
and crabs are laden with oil.
where now can i find my dreams?

was it an exercise only,
a preface to a holocaust?
how many have died?
were they mostly crazy?
did they lie in their own blood
choking on their new found freedom,
an ancient memory sheltered
and planted in you?
everyone says you were only a rehearsal.
a staging area with the actors
mad men and women
scattered through-out your foothills.
the directors, a few partitioned marxists
waving flysheets of rhetoric,
the producers, self-righteous capitalists
who find no industry more
profitable than war
and the cast of thousands
farmers, only, and children,
women and prophets,
builders of new beginnings.

why are your dead
flattened as troublesome flies
hidden from my eyes,
the rubble of your lives
edited from my knowing?

grenada you are more than a symbol,
sound stage, first take,
rough draft of a master plan.
you are flesh and promise.
you, the lighthouse that beckoned for me
to keep on struggling.
you that sweat africa and sang its
principles to your children.
you held my dreams and
made me know of tomorrows.
i cheered your victories
and drank deeply of your hopes.
i was nurtured by your harvests,
each child who was taught,
each mouth that was filled,
each road that was built.
you held my dreams so gently.

you spoke so softly, understood people
living in rhythm with time.
you faced terror, yet continued to grow,
resisted flight and capitulation.
you made all things possible
because of your human purpose.

now you lie wounded, tubercular spit
eating away at your lungs.
you cough up your families
in pieces on your beaches.
how can i save you, grenada,
who though small and poor
offered a bountiful harvest to so many?

where can i send my dreams, grenada,
now that you lie, the warm dark flesh
across your middle torn, open and yellowing,
your beaches covered with blood and tin cans,
a river of tears washing your streets?

*in 1983 under the direction of then president ronald reagan american forces invaded socialist grenada (the only country in the western hemisphere to have a successful bloodless revolution) under the pretext that the public vitriolic split between opposing marxist groups had caused the assassination of maurice bishop and turned the nation into a dangerous fascist state which threatened americans in a small medical school. the socialist government was overturned and an american selected leadership was put into place.

dm

RESISTANCE

when you count the fallen
this one person
this one black lady
will not have fallen.

when you count
those who quietly accepted
prisons of tears and madness,
king alfred's dreams of resettlement
color neutralization.
when you take the time to count
those who did not see the use for struggle
and those who could not find the time
when you find
the withered who lost the dream
the bent saplings who never found one
when you look for complacency
this one
here
will not be
in their number.

this one individual
refuses to throw up her hands
and wring them in despair.
in the face of odds
that call her dreams a long shot
this one person
plays to win.
sees time as a road
and travels it hard.
refuses to be
an unlisted causality of war
refuses to forget
refuses to be subdued
to find revolution
an armchair profession
or summer time fad.

this one person
will fight.
this one unmiracle maker
is going to be

a part of the dream
when it happens.
this one person
refuses genocide
will be a spirit catcher
will struggle for the dream
when the body fails
when the heart stops.
when you count the fallen
this one person
will not be
in their numbers.

dm

MUSIC

JAZZ ME

come jazz me
come jazz me
blow my trumpet
come play me
soothe me
strum my guitar

i am the music
you hear
echo
echoing from the ocean
i am the sound
that tingles
tingles in the wind
each time
your fingers near congo
drums

come jazz me
hum me
play me baby
i am the music
the rhythm
the beat in jazz
bebebebebopbopbop
bopbopbadap
bapbap
baa
totototadada
yeah

come jazz me
come jazz me
come jazzzzzz me
i'm here
bebebebebopbop
bapbap
totototadada

opa

DEATH AND RITUAL

they lay the bodies on steep mountainsides
letting vultures consume the flesh.

bodies are fed to the river,
where fish and algae absorb the remains
until the bones,
softened with time
sink to the sand
become home for minute carrion eaters.

logs are piled up the fire.
as the body burns the eldest son smashes
the skull so it cannot explode.

the bones, white, are fed
to river, mountain, earth
laid underneath a tree
the remains, shaken to the wind
forgotten in time.

women are not allowed near the body.
we weep, moan, pull the spirit back.
it must fly, fly through time
meeting itself at the rainbow's edge.

it is black
it knows no color
it rides a melody
a long clear note
blown from a smoke filled saxophone.
music to forever it becomes
bird, tree, star.

they do not allow us near.
women moan, cry too loud,
weep, remember too well.
only we can still the wind.

it rides the wind
a note blown through
a smoke filled saxophone
low, sweet caressing your heart.

life explodes from volcanoes
after the body perishes
becomes waves on the shore
after the bones bleach and turn to sand
it is rain that nourishes young blossoms
after the flesh has stopped turning colors
life is a note blown sweet, soft, low.

they do not allow women near.
women moan and remember.
wombs collapse upon our eggs
as we scream in blood.
women can stop the wind.

when the deed is done
by river, on mountains
in pyres heaped with wood
bought from men
whose hands you've never touched.

after the ritual is performed
the bones bleached soft, sand
ash that rides on the wind
the women come
and sing.

wombs remember life
cannot be created or destroyed.
it rides on the wind
on the soft sweet low notes
spun out of a smoke filled saxophone.

dm

LET THEM LAUGH

they laugh
i tell them
music has taste

miriam makeba is
smooth juicy cantaloupe
esther phillips
crunchy coconut
phoebe snow
sticky jam
odetta
is cucumber
nancy wilson
pungent orange
and roberta flack
she's a little
of all the tastes

they laugh
i say
these be my sisters
the women who
console me when
loneliness raps at my window
these be the sisters
i turn to when angered
by a system designed
to exclude us

they laugh
i tell it like it is
miriam has saved
my life
more than once
esther has given me
the shove i needed to
complete an assignment

yeah
my music has more
than a beat
it intuits
a sisterhood

that nurtures
protects
guides/advises

my music is the taste
of honey-bread, callaloo,
curried goat and strawberry ice cream

my music
sounds
when i need tenderness
emits force
when i need
to be bold
is pillow soft
when i need
rest
tender
when i need
loving

they laugh
i nod my head
at their ignorance
my music
embraces
is resistance
fights for peace
initiates/steps back
is laughing tears

hear the sorrowful pain
nancy bleeds in
guess who i saw today,
guess who i saw today...

dione,
he said he had to work
so i went to the show alone...
roberta,
Jessie, come home
there's a hole in the bed
where you slept
and now it's growing cold...

they laugh
i smile
turn up the volume
dim the lights
and be
young, gifted, and black

opa

FIRST SOUNDS

when i look
at you
music seeps
through my eyes
miles and his horns
in "sketches of spain"
reverberate to crescendo

when i
look
at you

your hand
on my thighs
returns the
5000lb man
rashaan roland kirk
takes us on a
journey
joy-filled
and magical
that place
eulipions
where i am
the only notes
you hum

when i
look
at you
heaven and earth
unite
and butterflies
dance the merenge

all the way
to bahia
we sail doing
the samba with grover washington jr.

i tell you
i look at you
i look at you

music fills my room
drums, cymbals,
horns and guitars
echo/resound
rashaan, miles, grover
miles, grover, rashaan
music
trembles/blends
i look at you
i look at you
notes fall from
your heart
i look at you
sounds bleed
from my belly
and i come

when i look
at you...

opa

HISTORY OF A 'MERICAN WORD

ja
ja ah
jazzy
jazz jazzy jazzing
jazzing
in dark rooms
shades pulled
sweat/skin
matted hair
fire sighs into morning
jaaaazzzzzz jaaaazzzzzzzing ja
aaaazzz children pinch
in special places
run hide swallow giggles
jazz jazzy smoke filled rooms
whorehouses with velvet walls
juke joints taunting
sunday church faithfuls
jazzing jazz
thick, warm scented
eyelids pulled low
people weave in time
moan jazz, in broken tar alleys
sharp metal piercing flesh
a violent rhythm
people weave jazz time
ja ah aaz
spilled love
spirals of sweat and perfume
spirituals touched
with african rhythms
struggles piercing eardrums
pumping the heart
awakening endless possibilities
jah aaz jazzing jazzy
ja ja
jah
jah
aaaaaaaazzzzzzzzz

dm

CHILDREN

CHILDREN WITHOUT CRIME

little black boys
have eyes that sing
with dreams and laughter.
pulse beats of today
little black boys
are explosions of life
slap hands in double time
somersault over narrow fire escapes
ease across splintered banisters
put robots and electricity
in a rhythmic perspective
as they turn on their heels and jut
out their chins.
little black boys
have eyes that sing
even in midnight shadows.

little black boys
are sometimes kissed while they sleep
blankets tucked around slim shoulders
smelling of soap and mama.
little black boys
are sometimes left alone
under darkness' cover to wake up
and think about how nice it will feel
when mama gets home and
offers breakfast as a celebration
of their ability to survive
one more night
little black boys nestled in corners
with toy guns and child faith
for protection try
to hurry up the sun.

little black boys
are sometimes left alone
by mothers whose hands are swollen
with patches and scales
of leftover memories
mothers who clean floors
with the sweat of unshed tears
wax them with prayers for their children.
little black boys hum lullabies

to themselves as they cradle plastic pistols
to ward off the monsters of their universe.
little black boys
who know that spiderman
won't come and save them,
somehow still hope
as they cry for a daddy
they hardly know.
little black boys
sometimes crouch in corners
not understanding the door
as it splinters towards them
chasing their lives
into sulfur, fire and dust.

little black boys
whose eyes sing laughter
even in midnight shadows
do not understand the blue and silver
that looms in front of them
blasting out ignorance
and gunpowder murdering
them in their innocence.
their eyes wet and edged with
white soft sleep are frozen
in terror as blood gushes
from their mouths
and washes the matted carpet
with death.

little black boys
with eyes that sing laughter
face death in midnight shadows
without shields.
little black boys
are warned
but not protected.
little black boys
who have no shields
are warned but not protected
little black boys
with eyes that sing
know death in midnight's shadow.

dm

BLACK WOMAN I

we thought it safe
because our soles treaded
on solid ground
soil of the same
mold from which
we were weaved
strength of the same
beauty that led us on
we thought it safe

but we've always known
there is no protection
for women of african roots
who have never been more
than a pussy
a hole for men to
sow their oats
practice on...

we thought it safe
even after we were bred
like horses
to ensure a pool
of slaves

we thought it safe
even after we
held the poisoned seeds
of their terrorization
and washed it clean
until it became flesh of
our flesh

we thought it safe
mother god
take me home
my feet know the road
of the ocean waves
mother god
take me home
my body knows the rhythm
of the threshing sea

we thought it safe
we who were entered
like bitches in heat
as we scrubbed
on our knees
their floors

groped at
as we packed
their clothes
starched with our hands

we thought it safe
as geritol men
in subways
on buses
brazen with
crooked smiles
grasped our knees
and fingers knuckled
and cold white
pulled our nipples

we thought it safe
when returning from work
laden with fatigue
we were pulled onto
concrete slab and hate
forced its way up
through   between   our thighs

we thought it safe
when we were not believed
what were you doing on the streets so late?
you know you liked it.
are you sure you didn't beg for it?

we are nasty freaks
who like to be pumped
anywhere, anytime
even by strangers
propelled by hate

we thought it safe
and had daughters

and send them out
alone
without daggers strapped
to their legs
without guns
hidden under their arms
without weapons
to hold themselves
we thought it safe

mother god
our noses
no longer smell
the belly of the ocean
yet we must walk
on the water

we thought it safe
when our daughters, sisters,
cousins, friends, aunty's mother
whispered her guilt

he touched me;
he made me touch him;
he grabbed me;
he brushed his hand over my breasts;
he sucked my pussy;
he stuck out his tongue at me;
he forced me; said i'd been teasing him,
that i'm horny; all i need is a good fuck..

we thought it safe
pretended not to hear
wore our shame like mourning
avoided each other's eyes
refused to listen
to the hushed voices marred with pain

we thought if
we ignored it
it would go away
that all we had to do
was wear loose dresses
sit with our legs tight
speak softly

remove all traces
of anger, rebellion
from our eyes
clean our nails
do not resist
do not resist
do not resist

we thought it safe
and in our pretense
disappeared into the
background
sisters will do anything for attention.
you know she was having a good time
and got caught.
shit ain't no one be rapin no black woman;
they be givin it away on the corner.
that's my bitch; ain't she fine.
that's my woman; and she's all mine.

we thought it safe
and i have birthed
one daughter
while another feeds
in my womb
and now i must teach them
how to hide the dagger
and where to plunge it
because i alone
cannot keep them safe
cannot keep them safe
cannot keep them safe
and i'll not
sacrifice them
like tawana*
tawana brawley, tawana brawley
child of my womb
tawana brawley
draped in my hue
tawana brawley

we thought you safe
tawana brawley
we media-rized your rage
tawana brawley

we thought you safe
tawana brawley
we feed you to the vultures
tawana brawley
we chastised you; made you cheap
tawana brawley
used and over looked
no justice for any of us

we thought it safe

*tawana brawley, a 15 year old black girl in upstate new york made the charge of rape over a 4 day period by six white men between november 24-28, 1988. she was found wrapped in a garbage bag, smeared with dog feces and the words "nigger" and "kkk" smeared over her torso. her case was thrown out on the grounds of lack of evidence

opa

CONVERSATION WITH MOTHER

be a good little girl.

i don't want
to sit with hands neatly
folded in my lap
legs together
waiting like sleeping beauty
to be rescued
there are no princes
in my world

*a young lady doesn't go
to the stadium to watch soccer.*

i didn't want to lie about
going to girl scouts' meeting
when all along i attended
soccer matches, chanting my winning
team to victory

but i had to be my own
kind of young lady
so i lied
yes i lied
and was proud
of myself
you had less anxiety
and i had big fun

why shouldn't i be
my own person
when that was all
i saw in you
you who defied
time and class boundaries
you who insisted on being
your own boss

ladies don't curse.

that's because they're stupid
afraid of their own power

someone mess with me i'm gonna
fight and curse them into next week

i observed your independence
that firm stride that stepped
into the middle of the most
volatile situation
and tackled the problem
to resolution

*nice girls don't
let boys touch them.*

i like the way
boys make me feel
when they tickle me
and their hands
accidentally brush
against my breast

i never wanted
to be a good little girl, mommy
never wanted to be a lady either
but i wanted to be
like you
to be who
you are

so i lied
and did what i
had to
to become
my own
kind of
woman

opa

CRACKER JACKS

step on a line you break your mama's spine
step on a crack you break your mama's...

what, tuff enough, engraved scowl,
fine scar across your eyebrow?
tight jeans, glazed eyes,
piled curses, spent daydreams
reeling in the sunlight
barely thirteen,
crack full, little girl
twenty dollar pebble in your pocket
ten dollar trick down the block.

lady bug lady bug, why do you roam?
your house is on fire and your children are home.

little girl, if you were my little girl,
i would take your face between my hands;
i would hold your eyes with mine;
i would look for the drop
the spark that was me,
when i fed you at my breast .
child, if you were my little girl,
i would remember
work my way down the cord
to see where it began to tear
so i could tie up each loose end,
feed your hunger with my love.

if you were my little girl,
if you were mine, child,
the rage would know no end.
and i would plead,

if i did not listen to you then
let me listen to you now.

i would hold you under
one arm and running, carry you
to the ocean of our knowing.

i would not let them take you away.
i would not let you become the blade

of the smoke you embrace,
reel, pull and puff,
puff again and call it home
and sunshine.
eeny meeny miney moe catch a

i would do all the wrong things
and maybe some of the right.

little girl, little girl
with your grown up habits
which eat smiles and devour lifetimes;
i would take you home.
more than holding up a mirror
i would make a door
kicking, pulling, flying
i would get you through
daughter if you saw what i see
when i look at you

*i'm a little acorn brown
laying on the cold cold ground
everybody steps on me
that is why i'm fractured, see...*

i see the benin bronze
almond queen mother's eyes
braids sweeping the neck.
i see nzinga curtsying to the
portuguese before proclaiming
there would be no slavery here;
holding spear, shield, and musket
to enforce her point.
i see the old woman, la vieja,*
the first one who bled this land
holding the spark as she held her breath
determining she and hers
i and i was gonna make it.
i see the pyramids
and i see cowrie shells
laying open in pairs.

pick a star
name it for yourself.
child i would take you home

and knead away the pain,
knead away the yearning.
i would bring you home
and this time,
this time
i would
teach you,
as i have begun to learn,
how to remember
what we felt like
when we were
truly free.

* the first africans brought to south america, who shared and taught their medicine and rituals of faith and power, were called la vieja when they became ancestors.

dm

WHAT WE GONNA DO 'BOUT DEM YOUTH?

dem don't know
dem don't see
dem do what dey see
dem do what dey know
dem don't know what dey do
dem don't see what dey eyes look through
dem eyes don't see what dey minds know
when dem gonna stop gettin' high and look
at what dey don't be seein'
and see what dey don't be knowin'
and know what dey got inside?
when dem gonna stop lookin' like
shiny magazine covers
slicked wet and smellin' of ink
dripped in white linen perfume?
when dem stop wantin' the gift wrappin'
and start wantin' the package?
when dem stop wantin' the package and
start wantin' to run the store?
when dem stop wantin' to be the storekeeper
stop wantin' to be all a the time
a buyer, a seller
a commercial of disposable lifestyles?
when dem gonna talk about breakin'
kola nuts with ogun?
when dem gonna squat
and drink rum with shango?
when dem gonna dance the night in yemoja
and comb dey hair with ivory from oshun
wrap dey limbs with cloth
from oya's leopard?
when dem gonna find dey power
take off the plastic dey mold onto their heads
dat seep into dey blood
so dey forget dey mamas, forget dey
papas, forget deyselves?
when dey gonna stop
bangin' dem hard heads
against dem electrified boxes of
won't-happen-fantasy?
dem is de promise
dem is de genius

dem is de love and de life
but dem got cotton balls soaked
with fragrant pods
stuffed inside dey ears
and dem feet got a hold
to a body snatcher that's
pullin' dem into a quicksand
of robots, death needles
and greased monkeys recitin'
computerized nursery rhymes.
dem sees sellin' dey bodies as a privilege
dem sees sellin' dey sisters as a profession
dem sees the mama and thinks her nuthin'
but a locked up heart
and an empty room of a future
dem sees the daddy and thinks him nuthin'
but a street walker
with a drug blanket memory
full of nameless women
droppin' they babies down
an endless well of forgetfulness
dem is de children
dem is de children of oludumare
dem is not chickens to be sacrificed and eaten
dem is not de beatin' of a sacred white goat
slaughtered and fed to obatala for justice
dem is touched by orunmila
dem is de children of africa
dem is not a babylon holocaust
a meanin'less rage
a self consumin' fire of hate
dem is ogun's shield
dem is shango's spear
dem is ochosi stalkin'
the jungle of nightmares
findin' the prey and severin'
the head of the monster
swift, silent, sure
dem is de beads
dem is de candles
dem is de love
dem is not a picture pasted on a billboard
tellin' dem how to fit in a box
die and be buried
at an early age gray and toothless

dem is de hope
dem is de dream
soon dem gonna take off dem glasses
with the backwards lenses
soon dem gonna look in de mirror
of dey days
and see demselves sittin' with nature
balancin' the planet on its head
soon dem gonna set the moon to spinnin'
and pull the earth into a righteous orbit
dem gonna see
dem is de today
dem is what's happenin'
dem is de promise of what will happen
dem gonna see
dem is de love
dem is de tomorrow
dem is de new
dem gonna look and do for demselves
dem gonna be de night
dem gonna be de stars
dem gonna see demselves
the new africa
the life
dem gonna take the universe
and make it sing.

dm

THE REAL BLACK BEAUTY

you are
everything
sweet   dark   rich
like molasses
sugar
before it crystallizes

you are
star-apple
purple and sweet
blackberries
purple grapes
ebony wood
durable   strong

you are charcoal
and the night
with its soothing
coat of darkness

you are everything
sweet
prunes   raisins
licorice
the seed of ackee
the soul which nourishes
life

you are the beauty
least talked about
the splendor
most often denied
because you are africa
the first
foremost

you are everything
that is primary
everything
that is nourished

you are
the core of life

dark
         splendid
                  enduring...

opa

LOVE

LONGING

tongue entwines air
to bring you home;
caresses silence
a rope of promises
float across dark
to bring you here
where there is
no profit but peace
no quiet through passion
few flatlands between
the mountain cliffs
we climb
yet,
galaxies emerge
when we come
together
here.

dm

LIVING/HATING

rattle of the furnace
cooling
sounds of breathing
silence of the night
you left
children no longer
rejoice
innocence is a looking glass
continuous yearning
spilling of soul
autumn when
laughter shined on our feet
the river was quiet
as we kissed
whispering
you in me
me in you

wishing a child
would rise in
my uterus to
torment you
let you choose
but i'm sensible
open about
what i want
afraid to gain what
i need

you come
i smile within
my breast
do you know
i already love
you for being here
night raps at the
bed for you
the mattress groans
your pleasure
my desire
the walls listen
embarrassed

i chastise myself,
speak of throwing
mockery in your face

but you know
i come,
listen for
your call
and go foolish

perhaps
i care
or maybe
i'm just
lonely

opa

LOVERS

not like lady,
ridges between where i am
where i choose not to be.
me, beyond newspaper collages -
you, beside all memory -
not like a lady
or even dame or whore
did i love you.
virulent and brown
tongue popping bubbles of heat
wrapped around ripe plums
lips seeping juice and smiles.
not ritual, smokey as dream.
wet, slapping, hot, and
not at all like form,
an ideal
the she that never was
only me, dipping with the city swing
streetcar wires, salty champagne
kinked in the pebbles of hot tar love
sand and ocean alive.
what a difference
myth
history
us.
a mirror
frame cracked
lake of laughter
ripples, ripples,
phases of the moon.

when we meet like this
i cry, simply
dance, breathe

*and if it don't fly
ain't nuthin' but a broken wing mendin'.*

dm

THE BEGINNING

let's agree
to be in the middle
of this

let's forget
the awkward
newness
the tentative
stares
the hesitant
clutches

we're in
the middle
remember
me free in your arms
your breath
pressed hot
on my back

i want
to live in
the gentle
fold of your arms
the familiar
belonging that makes
me direct your hand
to wetness

let's agree
to be in the middle
that we will be here
for each other
to germinate

opa

SHARING EVERYTHING

(to tarik)

i want to wash
you in my love
steal the sun
for our bed
deny day break

we have to begin
now
to discard
promises made
without vision
to welcome changes
that open room
for our love

i want to smell
you in all my rooms
reach out for you
and find you in
my favorite book
know that the space
i call home
is ours
that we nurture
the same dreams
that we can transform
our lives to be
two leaves
on a single stem

i want to bathe
myself in your fluid
cradle your head
to my groin
and die from
your love
i want you
home
with us...

opa

i want to swallow mornings with you
tenderly stroke the rivers
of sun filled afternoons
i want us to sip evening shadows
as i engrave your reflections
upon my soul.

dm

CLOSING

DAUGHTERS OF YAM: TRAVEL NOTES

everywhere we go strangers
whose noses are full
of the headiness of death
attempt to wrap terror
in thick blinding bandages
around our eyes.

everywhere
we go strangers recite
incantations, proclaim
that our family is not our own.
yet we know that
there are more maps to read
than people to hear.

we pierce ears
stretch lips
sifting across the news of today
discovering promise next to the pain
traveling women on the road
carrying the rich soil of africa
between our breasts.

everywhere we go
family stretches broadly
each time our languages meet
in the sweet water of the throat
where a shrug recalls birthplace
and a laugh means kinfolk
we have gotten sidetracked at times
but never were lost.

we unwrap the tissue of ignorance
bury our dead, mourn deeply,
move forward
and remember to remember
our harmony of bloodlines.

dm/opa

opal palmer adisa

devorah major

About the Authors

Opal Palmer Adisa, Jamaica born, is a poet, short story writer and playwright. Her poetry has been published in Jamaica, England and the U.S.A. Her plays have been performed in the San Francisco Bay Area. She is also a performance poet who combines music, slides and drama in the presentation of her work. Her published works are *Bake-Face and Other Guava Stories* (1986 - Kelsey St. Press, Berkeley, Ca.), *Pina, the Many Eyed Fruit*, (1985 - Julian Richardson Associate, San Francisco, California). Her daughter, Shola (Joy), continues to be the spark that drives her work.

Devorah Major is a California-born writer who works through poetry, short stories and essays. Trained in dance and theater. She is a performance poet who uses various art forms to enhance the power and presentation of poetry. Her work has been published in various magazines and anthologies including *Practicing Angels, California Childhoods, Pushcart XII, Black Scholar* and *River Styx*. She recently completed a book of poetry, *Combs and Cowries*, and a book of short stories, *Brown Glass Windows*. Her daughter, Yroko, and son, Iwa, inspire, enrich, frustrate and focus her work.

Both poets have worked together as Daughters of Yam since 1984, performing throughout Northern California with exceptional jazz musicians, visual artists, and, on occasion, dancers, as a part of the growing movement that seeks to bring quality poetry off of the page and make it a dynamic and accessible art form for more and more people.